BRADWELL'S IMAG

The Yorkshire Dales

BRADWELL
BOOKS

A TASTE OF THE YORKSHIRE DALES

REETH · KETTLEWELL · CHAPEL-LE-DALE · KILNSEY CRAG · DENT

Introduction

Welcome to **Bradwell's Images of the Yorkshire Dales** – a lovingly prepared collection of photographs that cannot fail to whet your appetite to explore the region for yourself, and that we hope will act as a constant reminder of the sheer beauty of The Yorkshire Dales.

Photographers, Susan & Andrew Caffrey, have a deep passion for The Yorkshire Dales and its delightful landscape; a passion that is clearly reflected in each of these unique and stunning images. The book is divided into nine distinct areas, each with a short introductory paragraph outlining its main features; however, we think the photographs really speak for themselves.

Enjoy!

Field path and gate at Muker

SWALEDALE

Gunnerside

Below Gunnerside Gill lies the small town of Gunnerside, an old mining town with fabulous walks, including access to the ever popular Coast to Coast path, gentle riverside routes through lush meadows, and for the more fearless, Pennine Way via the Tan Hill Inn, the highest pub in the country.

Looking from the start of the Buttertubs pass towards the village of Hawes

UPPER WENSLEYDALE

Hawes

At 850 feet above sea level, the market town of Hawes is the highest in England and beautifully situated between the mountains Buttertubs and Fleet Moss. Key attractions are the Dales Countryside Museum and the Wensleydale Creamery, where visitors can see the famous cheese being made in the traditional way.

Squeeze stile in the village

St Margaret's Church

Looking down on the village

Pointing the way above Hawes

Hardraw Force waterfall

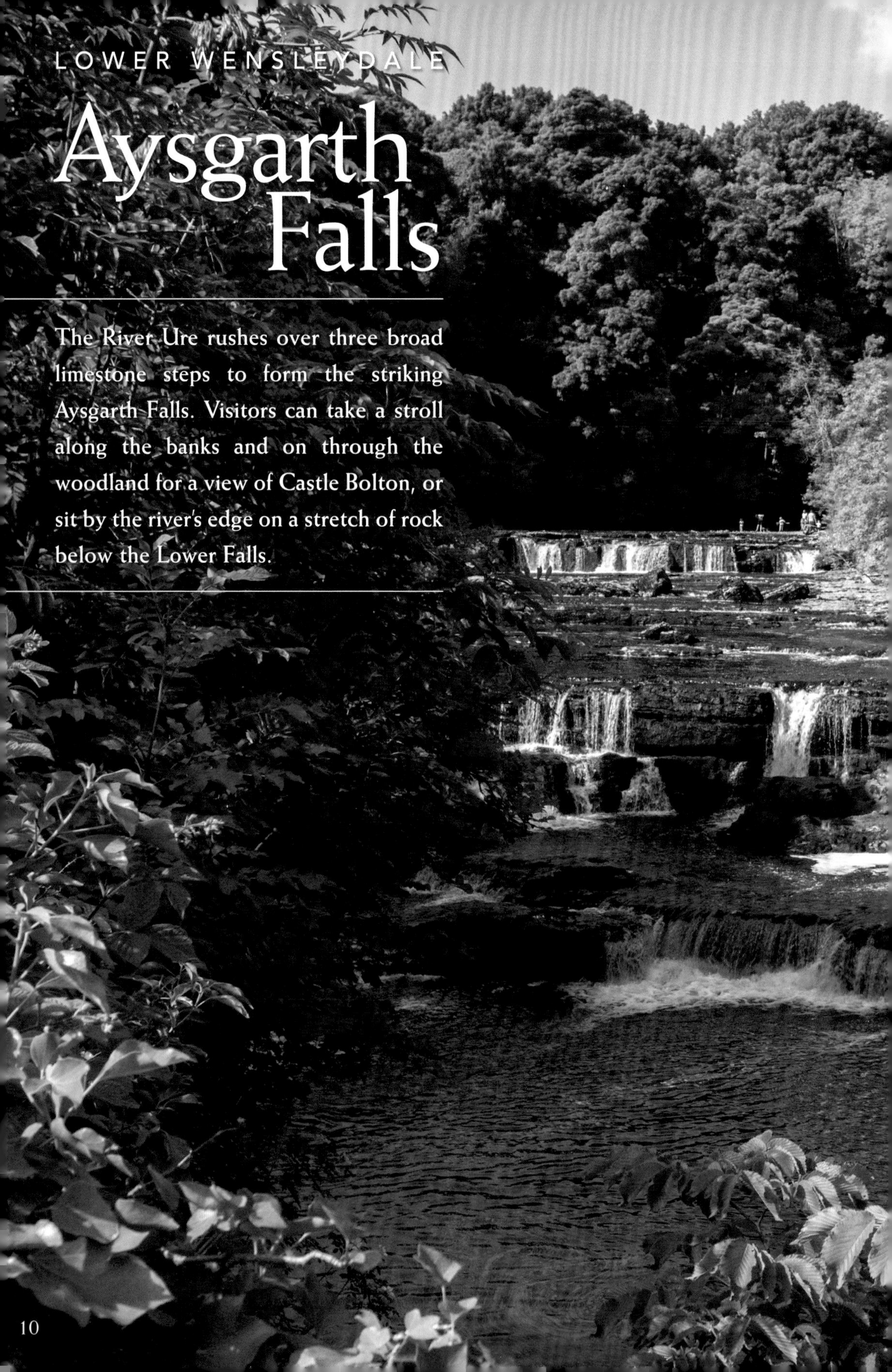

Aysgarth Falls

The River Ure rushes over three broad limestone steps to form the striking Aysgarth Falls. Visitors can take a stroll along the banks and on through the woodland for a view of Castle Bolton, or sit by the river's edge on a stretch of rock below the Lower Falls.

SWALEDALE

Muker

Muker provides an excellent starting point for discovering the fairest of North Yorkshire's valleys, Swaledale, via footpaths through open, flower-strewn meadows. The tiny village itself comprises a shop, a church, a tea shop with open fireplaces, and a welcoming pub, all against the fantastic backdrop of Kisden Hill.

Looking down the valley

Freshly mown farmers fields on the outskirts of Muker

Path leading to the river Swale

Limestone pavement at Malham cove

MALHAMDALE

Malham

Malham is a small, pretty village in the Pennines near to several breathtaking natural sites. Footpaths give access to Malham Cove, an imposing amphitheatre of limestone 260 feet high, and Gordale Scar, a colossal Ice Age gorge with a waterfall running through it that can be climbed in dry weather.

Malham cove

The entrance to Malham cove

The view from the edge of Malham cove towards Malham

An erratic boulder with Moughton Scar in the distance

RIBBLESDALE

The Norber Erratics

These 'erratic' sandstone boulders, some 430 million years old, perch precariously atop younger limestone to create one of the most remarkable landscapes in the Dales. Walkers regularly make the excursion up from nearby Austwick village to marvel at the uniquely contrasting stones, set in pleasant green walking country.

Burnsall

From the beautiful riverside village of Burnsall, holidaymakers are free to roam around the idyllic countryside of Lower Wharfedale. Dales Way runs the full length of Wharfedale via riverside paths and on towards the Lake District, while tougher routes lead up to the open access land of Barden Moor.

Ribblehead Viaduct

The majestic stone arches of Ribblehead Viaduct carry the Settle-Carlisle Railway over Batty Moss, towering over 100 feet above this remote and rugged landscape. The longest viaduct on the railway and a scheduled ancient monument, Ribblehead remains a popular landmark and walking destination for its stunning sights and fascinating history.

Hubberholme with 19th century gritstone bridge

UPPER WHARFEDALE

Hubberholme AND Yockenthwaite

These two tiny, picturesque hamlets are nestled in Langstrothsdale, where magnificent scenery abounds. A favourite local route follows Dales Way footpath from Buckden to the farming hamlet of Yockenthwaite, along the River Wharfe and on to Hubberholme, where the George Inn offers refreshments to weary walkers during spring and summer.

Yockenthwaite and the River Wharfe

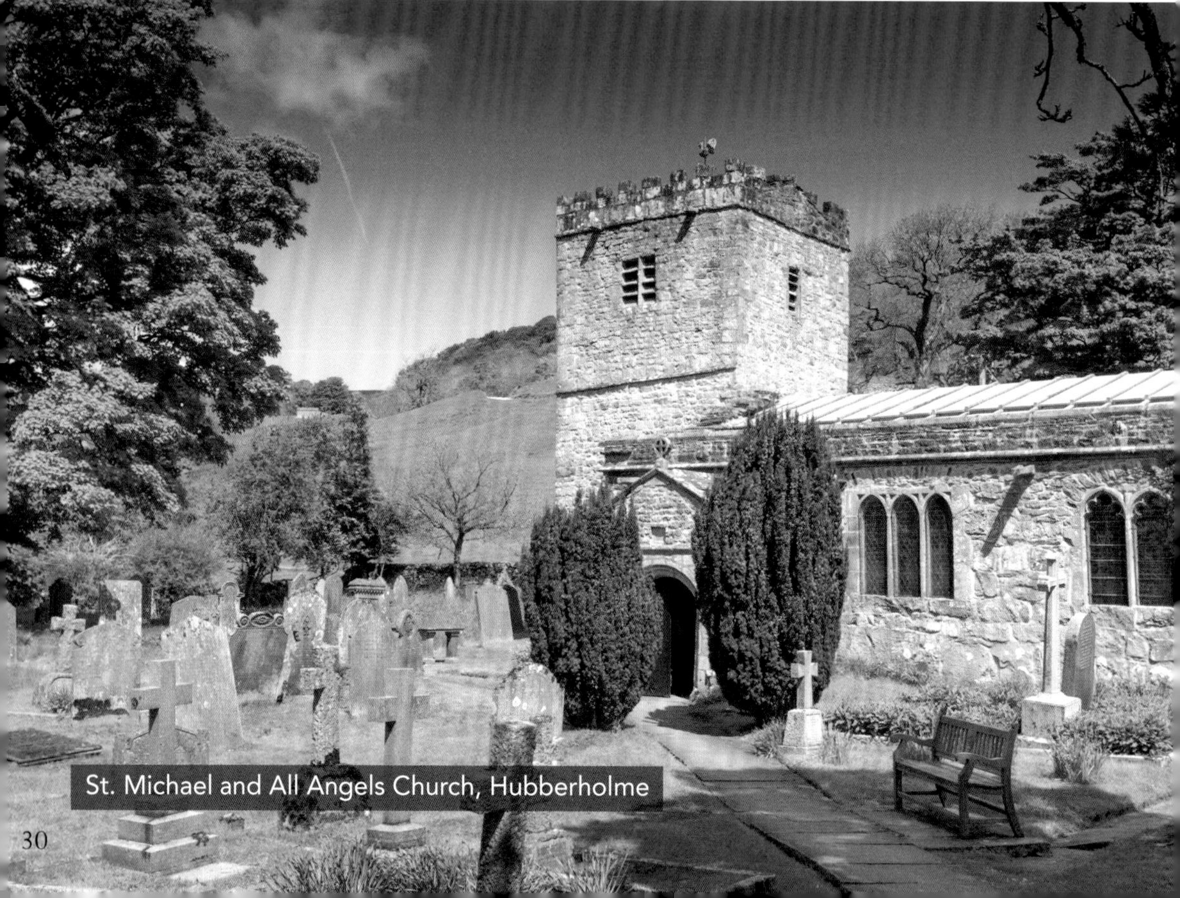
St. Michael and All Angels Church, Hubberholme

Yockenthwaite Bridge over the River Wharfe

A TASTE OF THE YORKSHIRE DALES

BOLTON ABBEY • PEN-Y-GHENT • APPERSETT • GRINTON • HORTON IN RIBBLESDALE